JIHAD JONES AND THE KALASHNIKOV BABES

BY YUSSEF EL GUINDI

★

DRAMATISTS
PLAY SERVICE
INC.

JIHAD JONES AND THE KALASHNIKOV BABES
Copyright © 2014, Yussef El Guindi

All Rights Reserved

SPECIAL NOTE

SPECIAL NOTE ON SONGS AND RECORDINGS

To Torange Yeghiazarian and Golden Thread Productions.

ACKNOWLEDGMENTS

I would like to extend my sincere thanks to John Eisner and the Lark for hosting a workshop of the play; to Torange Yeghiazarian and Golden Thread Productions for rolling the dice and giving it its first production; to Seth Rozin and InterAct Theatre, as well as Tina Parker, Christopher Carlos, and Kitchen Dog Theater for making it part of the National New Play Network's rolling world premiere. Additional thanks to Jeff Zinn and Wellfleet Harbor Actors Theater, David Gassner and Theater Schmeater, Laura Hope and Loyola University, and Sandy Harper and Richard Reichman at Cyrano's Theatre Company for giving it subsequent productions. (And thank you Sandy for encouraging me to write the following author's note for their production of the play.) Also to Robin Wright for devoting some pages to the play in her book *Rock the Casbah*.

AUTHOR'S NOTES

It's strange to find oneself part of a racial/ethnic/religious group that has been cast as villains on the world stage. Apparently auditions were held for lead villains and I wasn't even consulted. Suddenly — I say suddenly, though this has been happening for most of my politically-conscious life — I find myself having to account for the actions of a group of extremists I would never, ever consider hanging out with. Somehow I'm responsible for these violent idiots. Frequently I find my interactions with others involves this strange dance of both distancing myself from these few violent individuals/groups, who end up tarnishing the vast majority, while at the same time trying to provide a context for what's happening, without appearing to justify these awful deeds.

Of course, the question as to why a particular group gets singled out from a plethora of bad guys operating in the world at any one moment is an interesting question. Which leads to the debate about this notion of "manufactured narratives." Those stories that the mainstream culture keeps in play for whatever reason. One will hear (more in a subtle manner these days) that such-and-such a people are just somehow prone to violence. Or some other nationality will be labeled as lazy and shiftless. Or still another group will be said to be untrustworthy and sneaky, etc. And because we are all human, sharing similar traits, it's not hard to find news stories that confirm these negative stereotypes of people.

I think Carl Jung's idea of "projecting our shadows" onto others is key here. But that's a subject worthy of a whole essay, not here for these short notes. Plus, there is an additional discussion to be had about how these manufactured narratives serve certain political ends (note how the official narrative on Iran, for example, has shifted over the decades).

For these brief notes, I will say that being in the entertainment business, a business that will naturally take its cues from these mainstream narratives, it is doubly strange to have to navigate one's sense of self/identity through these misperceptions. Being a writer from a group that is currently occupying the role of lead villain, I have three options: I can either address these concerns directly, as I have in this play; or indirectly, as I have done in other plays; or I can ignore the whole vexing issue altogether, as I sometimes do, if just to take a break. But what if I was an actor of Middle Eastern descent who was being offered roles that bolster these negative stereotypes? What if the only parts being offered were these kinds of roles? What if I had a family to support and needed the money? Perhaps I could justify it by thinking that if I take on this "evil-doer" role it might lead to better, less stereotypical roles in the future. Or perhaps I can persuade myself that by taking on this hideously written "character," I can flesh him out, humanize him, and perhaps lessen the emotional damage it might do to that Arab kid who might watch the film.

The genesis for this play arose from years of being that Arab kid watching actors of Arab descent taking on these kinds of bad-guy roles. As I would sit there either cringing or enraged at these portrayals, I would think: what on earth persuaded these actors to take these parts?

Jihad Jones and the Kalashnikov Babes is my attempted inquiry into that question.

JIHAD JONES AND THE KALASHNIKOV BABES was produced by Golden Thread Productions (Torange Yeghiazarian, Artistic Director) in San Francisco as part of the National New Play Network's rolling world premiere, opening on June 5, 2008. It was directed by Mark Routhier. The set design was by James Faerron; the lighting design was by Jacob Petrie; the sound design was by Sara Huddleson; the costume design was by Sarah Al Kassab; and the production stage manager was Elizabeth W. Curtiss. The cast was as follows:

ASHRAF	Kamal Marayati
BARRY	David Sinaiko
PEGGY	Jessica Kitchens
CASSANDRA	Cat Thompson
JULIUS	Mark Rafael Truitt

As part of the National New Play Network's rolling world premiere, JIHAD JONES AND THE KALASHNIKOV BABES was subsequently produced at InterAct Theatre Company in Philadelphia and at Kitchen Dog Theater in Dallas.

The play was produced at Theater Schmeater (David Gassner, Artistic Director) in Seattle, opening on January 15, 2010. It was directed by Steve Cooper. The set design was by Michael Mowery; the lighting design was by Dave Baldwin; the sound design was by Teri Lazzara; the costume design was by DodiRose Zooropa; and the production stage manager was Sharon Adler. The cast was as follows:

ASHRAF	Zaki Abdelhamid
BARRY	Daniel Christensen
PEGGY	Michelle Flowers
CASSANDRA	Miriah Caine Ware
JULIUS	James Weidman

JIHAD JONES AND THE KALASHNIKOV BABES was produced at Wellfleet Harbor Actors Theater (Jeff Zinn, Artistic Director) in Wellfleet, Massachusetts, opening on May 25, 2011. It was directed by Robert Kropf. The set design and lighting design were by Ji-Youn Chang; the costume design was by Anne Miggins; and the production stage manager was Maureen Lane. The cast was as follows:

ASHRAF.. Paul Melendy
BARRY .... David Fraioli
PEGGY... Susan Gross
CASSANDRA...Stacy Fischer
JULIUS..Robert Kropf

JIHAD JONES AND THE KALASHNIKOV BABES was produced at Cyrano's Theatre Company (Sandy Harper, Artistic Director) in Anchorage, Alaska, opening on February 14, 2014. It was directed by Dick Richman; the set design was by Brian Saylor; the lighting and sound design were by Sierra Ileta; and the production stage manager was Marc Hess. The cast was as follows:

ASHRAF...Matt Iverson
BARRY .... Kevin T. Bennett
PEGGY..Jacqueline Manhattan
CASSANDRA....................................... Kelle June Korpi
JULIUS... Robert Pond

CHARACTERS

ASHRAF

BARRY

PEGGY

CASSANDRA

JULIUS

JIHAD JONES AND THE KALASHNIKOV BABES

Barry's office. Ashraf is reading a script. Barry is at his desk involved with some task, but also watching Ashraf's reactions. Ashraf opens his mouth. Closes it. He turns the page.

ASHRAF. *(Beat, reading from the script.)* "You filthy whore-mongering little American, die. I spit on you and your mother. I screw your mother. You pig. You puke-eating pig. Die." *(Ashraf looks at Barry.)*
BARRY. Yup. *(Ashraf turns back to the script.)*
ASHRAF. *(Reading another speech.)* "You think I care if your family die? I care only if they die too soon." Have you, um — read this?
BARRY. Uh-huh.
ASHRAF. All of it?
BARRY. Uh-huh.
ASHRAF. All of it?
BARRY. Have *you*? No, so don't jump to conclusions.
ASHRAF. Conclusions?
BARRY. Yes.
ASHRAF. You mean — conclusions?
BARRY. If I had to choose a word.
ASHRAF. What did I miss? The part where he turns into a hero?
BARRY. Yes, maybe.
ASHRAF. You're saying I missed that in the first ninety pages?
BARRY. I knew it. I knew it would just: *(Makes sound and gesture of something going over his head.)*
ASHRAF. You're kidding.
BARRY. Not with this script.
ASHRAF. This character? Mohammed? Turns into a hero? The guy who says, "Abdul, pass me the pliers," as he holds the grandmother by the throat?

BARRY. This is exactly why I wanted you to read it in my office because I knew you would utterly misread it.

ASHRAF. So there's a lot of nuance I missed?

BARRY. No, you see, sarcasm may be cute, but it's actually a career-killer.

ASHRAF. And playing Mohammed, the bug-eyed, psycho, sadist terrorist will put me in the big leagues?

BARRY. Is the "T" word ever used in the script? *(Ashraf looks at him, flabbergasted.)* Is it?

ASHRAF. Barry.

BARRY. No.

ASHRAF. If it looks like a duck, Barry.

BARRY. This is so not a duck, and it's certainly no turkey.

ASHRAF. How does he turn into a hero after dangling the four-year-old out the window? Rifle-butting the wife a few pages later. And then gathering all the family photos into the living room and pissing on them. Not to mention strapping dynamite to himself and threatening to rape the eighteen-year-old daughter and go off with a bang.

BARRY. Please note the sense of humor. Dark but present.

ASHRAF. And then leering at the seventeen-year-old son and wondering if he should bugger him instead?

BARRY. Clearly he's bisexual. I think that's interesting. Do you have a problem with playing a bisexual? You shouldn't. Sexual ambiguity would do your image good. Brando had it and so did James Dean.

ASHRAF. You're kidding.

BARRY. Wait till I tell you who's attached to the project.

ASHRAF. I'm not playing this.

BARRY. Who do you have wet-dreams about?

ASHRAF. I don't care.

BARRY. You'll wet yourself.

ASHRAF. I'm not doing it.

BARRY. Throw out a name.

ASHRAF. I mean it, Barry.

BARRY. Okay I'll tell you.

ASHRAF. *(Interrupting.)* I don't want to know! That's the problem: There's always a good reason to screw yourself and do the wrong thing. I'm sick to death of this junk. Jesus God, being an actor doesn't mean I have to be a total idiot. I also have to live with myself and not throw up when I think of what I've done. Why did you even show me this script?

BARRY. Because you haven't held one in two years.

ASHRAF. And in all that time, this is what you bring me?

BARRY. Also because you now have a rep as the "no man." The actor who will say no to a script before they've even finished offering it to you.

ASHRAF. Because of that one time when I turned down the part in *Jihad Jones and the Kalashnikov Babes?*

BARRY. Ashraf, my friend: what's the point of having principles if you're not around to show people you have any.

ASHRAF. Barry —

BARRY. *(Interrupting.)* Listen to what I'm saying.

ASHRAF. I have to face myself, *me*.

BARRY. You're an actor. You have to face the public, that's your job, and my job is to get you in front of them.

ASHRAF. I can't face anyone if I hate myself for what I'm doing.

BARRY. Stop, please.

ASHRAF. Where do you think the strengths I draw on to do my work come from? Not from feeling like shit for doing roles that suck and feeling like a total prostitute.

BARRY. I can name you a dozen actors who prostitute themselves repeatedly and do fantastic work. Who feel like shit on a daily basis and do work that blows you away.

ASHRAF. Not with roles that suck!

BARRY. Even with lousy roles because they're good enough to transform whatever they're doing into something magical. And I say you're that good. I say you can take this role, chew it up, and make this shit shine like nobody's else crap.

ASHRAF. Barry —

BARRY. I refute any charge of being over-the-top.

ASHRAF. Don't get on a roll.

BARRY. I'm not backing down with this one.

ASHRAF. I hate it when you do that because then I stop trusting you.

BARRY. I thought you were working on trust issues with your therapist.

ASHRAF. Have you read beyond the first five pages?

BARRY. The whole script, carefully, with more care than I usually do because I knew you would be Little Miss Manners about it.

ASHRAF. What exactly would I be transforming?

BARRY. Please read it as an actor and not as someone with a stick up his ass.

ASHRAF. Barry: This is bad English, wrapped around bad writing, wrapped around a hideous plot filled with God-awful stereotypes and enough cheese to put me off dairy for the rest of my life.

BARRY. Are you done? Because I know your outrage must feel good, but I wouldn't get off on it because a self-jerk with no place to put it does not a career make. I so know that when this film comes out and you're not in it, you will fire me for not having done everything I could to have changed your mind.

ASHRAF. *(Cold, not buying it. He holds out the script.)* Show me this switch when he becomes all likeable and chummy.

BARRY. I didn't say that.

ASHRAF. When he becomes the "hero."

BARRY. "Hero" is an iffy term these days, that's the heart of this film.

ASHRAF. Where is the point where he stops being the most hideous thing on screen. *(Flips through the script.)* At the end? In the next few pages? He's not even here. One moment he's … *(Freezes on a passage. Slight beat, then, reading in a deadpan manner:)* "With his hands now trapped in Mr. Slinky, and wedged between the doorjamb and the pram, Mohammed is momentarily immobilized. Which gives Roger enough time to revive and reach for the shotgun. From his position on the floor, Roger angles the shotgun and shoves it up between Mohammed's ass cheeks. Roger turns to Heather: 'Sweetie: you may want to look away and cover your ears.' Heather: 'Daddy: I'd like to watch.' Betty enters with her arms around the twins: 'I think we all want to watch this.' Roger: 'Alright, but put on the goggles.' Mohammed: 'Fuck you and the American pussy that shit you. You all bitches.' Roger cocks the gun. Roger: 'Hey, Mo: kiss the virgins for me.' He fires, blowing a hole up through the top of Mohammed's head. Mohammed's body crumples, glancing against the mechanical monkey with the toy cymbals as he hits the ground, switching it on. The twins rush into their father's arms. Tears well up in Roger and Betty's eyes as they reach out to each other. The twins: 'Way to go, Dad.' As the camera pulls away with the family hugging each other, we can now make out that the monkey's cymbals are playing 'The Star-Spangled Banner.'" *(Slight beat.)*

BARRY. Yup. *(Slight beat.)* Knowing you, you're not going to see beyond what's on the page. You'll take it completely for what it seems without giving a thought it might be something else. *(Ashraf drops the script and heads for the door.)* Something that might be even more lucid and daring than you can imagine. *(Ashraf tries to*

14

open the door but it won't budge. He tries again.) That could change everything you want changed. But no, you're going to walk away.

ASHRAF. It's locked.

BARRY. You're so obvious you *are* a stereotype without even having to play one.

ASHRAF. The door is locked.

BARRY. Yes it is.

ASHRAF. Can you unlock it.

BARRY. No.

ASHRAF. Give me the key.

BARRY. Nope.

ASHRAF. Barry.

BARRY. No.

ASHRAF. *(Moving towards him.)* Give it to me.

BARRY. I care enough about you that I'm not going to open that door.

ASHRAF. Care for me?

BARRY. You the actor. You who should have had your name above the title years ago. I care for *that*, that's what I hold dear.

ASHRAF. Give me the key.

BARRY. *(Takes out key from pocket.)* This key? *(Ashraf reaches out to grab it; Barry avoids him.)* This little key is the key to everything you've ever wanted but are too gutless to grab. And I will not have cowards for clients. *(Ashraf moves again to grab the key. But Barry throws the key into an open box — perhaps a cigar box — and locks the box. Then Barry takes the box and puts it in his brief case. He locks the brief case. Ashraf, stunned, looks on. For good measure, Barry then opens a desk drawer, slides the briefcase in, and locks that. Ashraf stares at Barry. Then moves to the window.)* I wish to remind you my office is now on the fourteenth floor. And though your plunging career might yet survive your suicidal choices I'm pretty sure your body won't have the same bounce.

ASHRAF. How much are they paying? Will your percentage be a little higher?

BARRY. Nothing to do with that. You can be so smarmy when you get righteous.

ASHRAF. *(Approaching, somewhat threatening.)* What are they offering, Barry?

BARRY. No. Because then you'll think I'm operating solely· from financial consideration when there's a lot more at stake than the

15

enormous amount of money we'll both be paid. I've blocked it out myself because I didn't want that excitement to interfere with your decision as an artist.

ASHRAF. How much?

BARRY. Awe-inspiring, if you want to know. Just saying the number is like a full-body massage. I repeat it and this amazing sense of inner calm floods me. I thought they were talking about another actor when I first heard it.

ASHRAF. Give me a figure.

BARRY. What does it matter if you're not going to do it?

ASHRAF. I want to know what's making you want to shove this putrid crap down my throat.

BARRY. Well okay, let's see. *(Reaches for a calculator on his desk.)* How much are you getting paid in this play you're in now, what's it called?

ASHRAF. *Hamlet.*

BARRY. Twenty dollars a week?

ASHRAF. Two hundred.

BARRY. Oh my God: ten per cent of two hundred, excuse me while I book a vacation to Tahiti. Alright: let's figure this out. *(Punches in numbers.)* Two hundred dollars a week, times: a run of six weeks, minus ten percent, taxes; the number of wasted hours in rehearsal, not to mention the number of lines per minute and mind-numbing drudgery seven nights a week. No perks, no trailer, not even catering. What kind of life are you choosing for chrissakes!

ASHRAF. *(Through clenched teeth.)* It's called *theater.*

BARRY. It's a dungeon for out-of-work actors waiting for their lives to start in film.

ASHRAF. I want a fucking number.

BARRY. Eight hundred thousand dollars. I think I can push it up to a million. The film is budgeted for ninety million. *(Ashraf appears immobilized. Slight beat.)* It's astonishing the effect large numbers have. Especially with dollar signs attached. And in the end what does it mean? Apart from, you know, everything.

ASHRAF. Eight hundred thousand?

BARRY. A million. I'm pretty sure I can negotiate up. You *are* the second lead. *(Slight beat; looking at his calculator.)* That's about five thousand times more than you're making now. For three weeks' work. A million dollars for three weeks' work. *(Slight beat.)* Feel free to express joy. I won't tell anyone.

ASHRAF. That is so offensive.

BARRY. Which part? Paying your rent regularly? Not having to crash with your parents? Which totally undermines the integrity thing by the way.

ASHRAF. A million?

BARRY. Pow, huh?

ASHRAF. They're going to pour the entire budget of some poor city into *this*? *(Picks up script.)* Barry: I'm holding a hundred and twenty pages of toilet paper.

BARRY. You have to give it to movies: The dumber they get, the richer people become. Though this movie is far from dumb.

ASHRAF. Don't you ever think about what you're doing? Barry? What you're going to leave behind? I mean it, look at me. You are participating in the pumping of crap into the world. You are a polluter. *(Responding to another dismissive gesture or expression.)* I'm not getting on a high horse here. I'm talking to you as a regular person who has to walk out into the same world where this ka-ka is brought to life. Which people like *you* bring to life, and me, when I don't have the balls to say no because a million dollars would mean everything.

BARRY. You're saying yes?

ASHRAF. *No.*

BARRY. Well good. I'd be disappointed if you said yes to mere money, even though you'd be able to establish your own theater and pump out, you know, jewels of enlightenment to the two people in your audience.

ASHRAF. *No.*

BARRY. Do you realize the worst film of last year was seen by more people world-wide than the absolute best play ever staged in the past five hundred years. Wrong business? You're in the only business that matters for an actor.

ASHRAF. But why can't I be tempted by a brilliant script? *(Anticipating Barry's response.)* Talk to me, Barry; speak to me like I'm a human being and not a client to be pitched at. You *know* what this is.

BARRY. I do. Which is why I'm not letting you walk away. *(Looks at his watch.)* I wasn't moved to the fourteenth floor because I steered my clients wrong. *(Moves round to his desk.)* When you re-read it, you'll get it. And all these concerns you have of maligning your precious little constituency and shaming Semites everywhere will fade away. Unfortunately you can't do it now.

ASHRAF. What do you mean?

BARRY. We have a meeting.

ASHRAF. What meeting?

BARRY. *(Pressing the intercom.)* Peggy? *(Peggy is heard through the intercom.)*

PEGGY. *(Voice.)* We're on it.

BARRY. Where is he now?

PEGGY. *(Voice.)* He's in the restroom.

BARRY. Which floor?

PEGGY. *(Voice.)* Sixteenth.

BARRY. What's he doing?

PEGGY. *(Voice.)* Peeing?

BARRY. I mean is this a break or is the meeting with Cantwell over?

PEGGY. *(Voice.)* Cantwell's in there with him. Bob's monitoring.

BARRY. Where?

PEGGY. *(Voice.)* Outside.

BARRY. Tell Bob to walk in casually and enter a stall. Tell him to take up a position seated with his trousers down. I know Cantwell, he'll check. And no use of cell phones while he's in the stall.

PEGGY. *(Voice.)* I'm not comfortable asking Bob to take down his pants.

BARRY. Just do it and tell me what he overhears.

PEGGY. *(Voice. Whisper.)* OhmyGod.

BARRY. What?

PEGGY. *(Voice.)* Cassandra Shapely just walked by.

BARRY. Is she coming here?

PEGGY. *(Voice.)* She's asking … she's heading for the restroom.

BARRY. Which one?

PEGGY. *(Voice.)* She's taking the elevator.

BARRY. She's going up to sixteenth. She's pissed. She shouldn't have been kept waiting.

PEGGY. *(Voice.)* She is *such* a hottie. I swear to God if I wasn't straight.

BARRY. Absolutely do not make our guests uncomfortable. I will not have potential clients subjected to the fantasy lives of our staff. Now get on the phone and tell Bob.

PEGGY. *(Voice.)* I'm on it.

ASHRAF. *(Impressed.)* Cassandra — Shapely's — here?

BARRY. Yup.

ASHRAF. Is she — changing agents?

BARRY. Nope. But this agency is putting the package together.

ASHRAF. What package? *(Barry looks at him, waiting for the realization to hit. Beat.)* No.

18

BARRY. Yah.

ASHRAF. This — this film?

BARRY. Uh-huh.

ASHRAF. *This* film?

BARRY. Sounds better already doesn't it. Makes you wonder if it's not so bad after all.

ASHRAF. No way.

BARRY. It's true.

ASHRAF. She wouldn't slum like that. Not for this.

BARRY. Guess which part she's playing?

ASHRAF. I don't believe it.

BARRY. Sherry. The rebellious daughter who forms a bond with Mohammed. Who falls for him in a Patty Hearst-like moment of lust and politics. Your scenes, as you may have noticed, provide the film's erotic charge. You two will provide the biggest bang on screen since what's-their-names did in that film with the sea otter.

ASHRAF. Who's in the restroom? *(Barry looks at him smugly.)* Barry.

BARRY. You don't want to know. You said so.

ASHRAF. Who's in the restroom?

BARRY. I wanted to tell you but no, you don't want to do the wrong thing, "save me," fine.

ASHRAF. Just tell me.

BARRY. What director working now would you agree to play a cockroach for? In a sea of cockroaches, never mind the second lead in a film?

ASHRAF. Who?

BARRY. Begins with a "J." *(Slight beat.)*

ASHRAF. Julius. *(Barry maintains his smug stance.)* Is it Julius?

BARRY. Julius you say?

ASHRAF. *Barry.*

BARRY. Uh-huh.

ASHRAF. It is?

BARRY. Yes.

ASHRAF. Julius Steele?

BARRY. Mr. S.

ASHRAF. *(More incredulous.) Julius Steele?*

BARRY. There's only one. The big "J."

ASHRAF. *Wages of Sin* Julius Steele?

BARRY. *The Weight of Our Marrow* Julius Steele. *The Goldilocks Trilogy, The Flight of the Cocks* Julius Steele, yes, him, that one, the big guy. Against whom all other directors could only hope to have a sliver of his success. Now tell me I'm blowing smoke. Tell me I'm some sleazy agent trying to sell you down the river for a measly buck or two. Fuck you, okay. Julius Steele. In this building. Pissing, next to Cantwell. And when Cantwell's in the restroom with you pissing let me tell you: You don't stand next to Cantwell in the *pissoir* unless the package is done, and it's done. This agency is putting the next Julius Steele film together.

ASHRAF. *(Dazed.)* Oh no.

BARRY. We've got the juice right here.

ASHRAF. Oh God.

BARRY. This agency is moving up to a whole new level. Express elevator.

ASHRAF. Not him.

BARRY. Didn't I tell you?

ASHRAF. We're doomed.

BARRY. That's why I'm so pumped.

ASHRAF. I had no idea he hated us.

BARRY. Hated what?

ASHRAF. *(More to himself.)* Why else would he do a script like this unless he despised us.

BARRY. Ashraf. Change therapists. Wake up and smell the celluloid.

ASHRAF. This is horrible.

BARRY. There are no victims here, just winners.

ASHRAF. Why is it the people I admire the most are the ones who harbor these feelings in the worst way.

BARRY. Let me tell you something. —

ASHRAF. *(Interrupting.)* It isn't paranoia when there's proof!

BARRY. Do you think Julius Steele, the guy who cut his teeth doing documentaries on every known genocide and ones you've never heard of; who took time out for the sake of people's health to do public service spots on the digestive tract and changed *my* diet; do you think a guy like that would *stoop* to do a film that debases *anyone?* The Pope could learn from this guy.

ASHRAF. Barry, it happens all the time.

BARRY. Oh give it a break.

ASHRAF. People you think would have a clue, who you so admire you couldn't imagine they wouldn't share the same values —

BARRY. *(Interrupting.)* I don't want to hear this.

ASHRAF. *(Continuing.)* — you discover they have this one blind

20

spot and it happens to be you. Like Carl Jung. The founder of the therapy I've always gone to. He thought Arabs were lower than donkeys. Do you know what that did to me? Baring my issues to a Jungian and then discovering the founder would have felt contempt for me? How that affected my little problem of sensitivity bordering on paranoia which I admit I'm prone to? It left me feeling like the whole world's out to get me, *including my therapist!*

BARRY. Fuck Carl Jung. He's not directing the film.

ASHRAF. It could be anyone, *that's the point.*

BARRY. This ain't anyone.

ASHRAF. Even Julius Steele.

BARRY. Not our Julius; a guy who's been called the Thomas Jefferson of film.

ASHRAF. Thomas Jefferson had slaves.

BARRY. Oh bite me. You're doing this film. *(Into the intercom.)* Peggy?

PEGGY. *(Voice.)* We're on it.

BARRY. Where are they now?

PEGGY. *(Voice.)* They haven't left the restroom.

BARRY. Good sign. Keep monitoring.

PEGGY. *(Voice.)* I think I'm in love.

BARRY. Keep it in your pocket. *(During the above, Ashraf has picked up the script and turned to a page.)*

ASHRAF. Tell me, please, what is Jeffersonian about the opening scene of this film. Where you have Arab thugs bursting in on an American Thanksgiving dinner. Where the first thing Mohammed does after wrenching the grandmother's neck is stick his hand into the turkey, scoop out all the stuffing, throws it, and then forces the entire family to lick it off the floor. Paying special attention to the nubile teenage daughter as she bends down to do it.

BARRY. What strikes you about that scene?

ASHRAF. What strikes me?

BARRY. What comes to mind?

ASHRAF. It's hideous! It's beyond hideous, it's an incitement to riot.

BARRY. Thank you. I have one word for you, it's not complicated, you ready? Satire. *(Ashraf looks at him dumbfounded.)* Ring a bell?

ASHRAF. Satire?

BARRY. That's the word.

ASHRAF. *Satire?*

BARRY. With so many degrees coming out of your ass, you'd think one of them would mean you could read.

ASHRAF. You're kidding me.

BARRY. Nope.

ASHRAF. This is satire?

BARRY. That's why it's going to rock.

ASHRAF. What are you *on*?

BARRY. You can't see it because you're too emotional.

ASHRAF. That's what they see when they read this?

BARRY. You missed the point when you sped through it.

ASHRAF. *This*, what's happening to me now, this is satire. What you're trying to do to me is satire.

BARRY. This Carl Jung had a point, donkeys could get this.

ASHRAF. Satire, my ass.

BARRY. That's why it's so over-the-top! It's meant to be revolting and so bad you go, "Oh come on!" "Hands tied up with Mr. Slinky," "scooping out all the stuffing," "kiss the virgins," oh Jesus, wake up. Hasn't it occurred to you that nobody would be so off the scale of dumb that they would buy this?

ASHRAF. What are you talking about? People swallow this crap all the time.

BARRY. Not anymore.

ASHRAF. Now more than ever.

BARRY. We've moved beyond that.

ASHRAF. What world are you living in?

BARRY. Stereotypes are passé.

ASHRAF. What?

BARRY. We're done with that. Nobody does stereotypes anymore. We're living in a post-stereotypical world.

ASHRAF. What are you — ? People always want bad guys; it's human nature.

BARRY. I understand you may be so deep in victimhood that you can't distinguish a real cause from one of your crazed out-to-get-me fantasies.

ASHRAF. Have you switched on the news lately?

BARRY. We set a higher standard here. *(Ashraf's mouth opens suggesting a slew of retorts but Barry continues.)* Audiences are too savvy now to buy the type of blackface bullshit you think this film pushes. Stop being so arrogant you little shit. You can't be more ethical than Julius Steele.

ASHRAF. Where's the satire, Barry?

BARRY. I'm not going to recommend you if you're this dull.

ASHRAF. Where is it?

BARRY. Think about it.

ASHRAF. If it's a satire, there's a target, what's the target?

BARRY. That's right, what is the target?

ASHRAF. I'm asking.

BARRY. And you look down your nose at *me*?

ASHRAF. Barry!

BARRY. The family! It's the family. You idiot. Who else is in this picture? Do you think Julius Steele gives a rat's ass about anything less? About Arabs? Stop being so self-centered. Nobody gives a damn about your issues.

ASHRAF. The family?

BARRY. *Yes.*

ASHRAF. He's satirizing the family?

BARRY. The family, the American family. He wouldn't concern himself with anything less; that meaty, that important.

ASHRAF. *(Not buying it.)* Why is he satirizing the family?

BARRY. I'm not going to give you a lesson in reading.

ASHRAF. Why would he satirize the family, Barry?

BARRY. If you spent two seconds vacationing out of your ass you might discover what's actually around you, and that *maybe* the director is coming on board to address the very concerns you care about. Like justice, fairness, and all that other sissy shit which I respect except when you're being a prima donna about it. The family! Of course it's the family. Look at what happens. It's on every page: The overconsumption, the excesses, the mindless gluttony. A family with enough food on their table to feed hundreds. And how that — . I mean look at what it's saying. The way that turns us into a plundering machine that has to bully the world to keep our tables full and our bellies stuffed and how that blows back into our homes in an oh-so-ironic way. The whole film is an indictment of that! The monkey playing "The Star-Spangled Banner," for chrissakes. Should there be footnotes for you? The *(Makes quotation marks.)* "bad guys" who burst in are the "provocateurs." They trigger the issues Julius wants to tackle. I'd bet a percentage point he has a little twinkle in his eye for these thugs because they're the ones who help him get into the heart of this film. Through them we get the wake-up call. "Change or else." "Stop being the greedy, bloated, ugly American or suffer the ax of hubris and die." Think *Dr. Strangelove.* Think Kubrick. Think anything but what you're thinking because it's just *plain wrong. (Slight beat.)* And even if this film was everything you think it is, you should be fucking grateful you were asked to play a stereotype in a Julius Steele film. He would be on your resumé for the rest of your life. Your ingratitude, *that's* what's offensive. I swear to God I'm ready to recommend another actor.

PEGGY. *(Voice.)* Mr. Barkley.

BARRY. *(Into the intercom.)* What?

PEGGY. *(Voice.)* They've left the restroom.

BARRY. What's the word?

PEGGY. *(Voice.)* It's a go if they like Ashraf. Steele and Shapely are coming down to check him out. You'll never guess what Cassandra did?

BARRY. Where are they right now?

PEGGY. *(Voice.)* The elevators.

BARRY. What did she do?

PEGGY. *(Voice.)* She barged right in, stood between them, and told them to zip it up. Balls, Mr. Barkley. Beauty and balls. How much more can you pack into a woman.

BARRY. Let me know when they reach this floor.

PEGGY. *(Voice.)* I'm so on it. *(Barry and Ashraf look at each other.)*

ASHRAF. *(Slight beat.)* You're saying I'm …

BARRY. *Yes.*

ASHRAF. Totally off about this?

BARRY. *Believe it.*

ASHRAF. And if I was to … re-read it slowly, I would … see what you just said about…?

BARRY. *Look who's on board.*

ASHRAF. *(Slight beat.)* It really is some — radical approach? And won't leave me feeling like I betrayed everything?

BARRY. Do the words "reading between the lines" mean anything to you?

ASHRAF. Why does he want me?

BARRY. He saw you in that pompous play you were in. Thank God it was good for something.

ASHRAF. He saw me play Hamlet and wants me for *this*?

BARRY. Does that give you an idea of the type of depth he's envisioning for this role? *(Ashraf looks hard at Barry trying to make a decision.)* That's it, you're in. We're done. We have to tidy up. You will not show any hesitation when this man enters, do you understand. *(Into the intercom.)* Where are they now? — *Peggy?*

PEGGY. *(Voice.)* What?

BARRY. Where are they?

PEGGY. *(Voice.)* In the elevator.

BARRY. Pay attention.

PEGGY. *(Voice.)* I'm trying to find my lipstick. I represent this agency as well.

BARRY. Stop being such a tart and let me know when you see them. *(To Ashraf.)* Help me tidy up. *(Barry runs around straightening the office, as Ashraf sits down and leafs through the script.)* Look at this mess.

ASHRAF. *(More to himself.)* This really is a — satire?

BARRY. Get up. Get up. *(Ashraf rises from the chair; Barry adjusts it and the one opposite.)*

ASHRAF. Because if it — if it is, it's going to be ...

BARRY. Would you put the script down and help.

ASHRAF. Because if it's not, Barry, you don't understand. I would never — I would never be able to show my face to my family, or friends, ever again.

BARRY. Your parents would kick you out if they knew you hesitated. Now help me! *(At this point, Barry is carrying a pile of magazines to a desk drawer. A couple drop to the floor, which Ashraf distractedly picks up.)*

ASHRAF. If it's really everything you say it is ... It would just ... *(Handing him the magazines.)* be — mind-blowing. I mean that would mean he's ... *(Barry's attention is caught by the magazine's cover.)* more of a mensch than I —

BARRY. *(Showing him the cover of a* Playboy *magazine.)* Would you look at that. Huh.

ASHRAF. I had no idea she'd done a spread.

BARRY. Look.

ASHRAF. Oh. Wow.

BARRY. *(Has opened it to the centerfold.)* That isn't Photoshopped. That's all Cassandra.

ASHRAF. Why would she do that? She doesn't need the publicity.

BARRY. Ms. Shapely knows a career move when it stares her in the face. — What a face. *(They both stare at the centerfold photo.)*

ASHRAF. She has an astonishing ability to carry her nakedness well and still convey meaning.

BARRY. I'd love to play a stereotype having to manhandle her. Did I mention she has a habit of falling in love with her leading men?

PEGGY. *(Voice.)* The elevator doors have opened and they're walking down.

BARRY. *(Throws magazine into drawer, moves towards the door.)* Alright: be casual and don't fawn. You can be reverential, but in an off-handed way. Don't jabber or offer your opinions unless asked, and *never* question the integrity of this man's vision. And if I make this signal: *(Makes some sort of hand gesture.)* it means kiss ass right away.

ASHRAF. Barry. The key.

BARRY. What? *(Tries the door, it's locked. Hurries to his desk as he reaches into his jacket.)* On the other hand, you should maintain *some* dignity for the sake of this agency, even while sucking up unless I make this signal: *(Makes another hand gesture.)* which means dump dignity and grovel with all you've got. Where's the key? *(Barry searches one pocket, then the other.)* What did I — ? *(Frantically goes through his pockets.)*

ASHRAF. You put it in your pocket.

BARRY. I had it.

ASHRAF. Have you tried inside your jacket?

BARRY. *(Patting down his jacket.)* I was just playing with it. *(Opens desk drawers and looks, taking out a few things, including the* Playboy *magazine.)* Where — ? … Shit. Shit. *(Into the intercom.)* Peggy.

PEGGY. *(Voice.)* They've stopped to talk to Brian.

BARRY. Get your office key and open my door. We've locked ourselves in.

PEGGY. *(Voice.)* Why did you do that?

BARRY. Just do it.

PEGGY. *(Voice.)* I gave it back to you.

BARRY. What?

PEGGY. *(Voice.)* You told me to. When we — almost had that tryst? That never happened because you thought it would lead to a pay raise.

BARRY. Jesus Christ.

PEGGY. *(Voice.)* Why did you lock yourself in?

BARRY. Who else has a key?

PEGGY. *(Voice.)* Just you.

BARRY. *Jesus God.*

PEGGY. *(Voice.)* Have you tried your shoes? You've hid stuff there before. *(Another phone rings. Barry picks it up, ticked off.)*

BARRY. What? *(Change in tone.)* Mr. Cantwell. Yes. — That's … that's great. *(Takes shoes off to check. Perhaps a small packet of powdery stuff falls out, which he quickly pockets.)* Oh Ashraf's very excited. Loves it. Very much onboard. *(Barry empties his pockets: we see two sets of keys, two cell phones, and other assorted gadgets.)* I promise you, Ashraf will not screw this up for us. *(Barry also picks up a box of tissues and turns it upside down. Then he takes out clumps of tissues, some of which fall onto the open* Playboy *issue, which he then closes.)* Really? — She looks great in *Playboy.* — No kidding. Regrets it, huh. Not a problem. I won't mention it. We won't even say the word "naked." Alright Mr. Cantwell. *(Dips his hand down his crotch to make sure it hasn't slipped there. He unzips his fly and goes in from there.)* Yes. I understand. And my family's life as well. I love you too. Bye. *(The place looks a little more disheveled now.)* WHERE IS THE FUCKING KEY?

ASHRAF. Perhaps it's a sign.

PEGGY. *(Voice.)* Mr. Barkley?

BARRY. Where are they?

PEGGY. *(Voice.)* About thirty feet and approaching.

BARRY. Stall them.

PEGGY. *(Voice.)* How?

BARRY. Improvise.

PEGGY. *(Voice.)* Make a scene, you mean?

BARRY. *(Taking hold of the desk drawer and tugging.)* Do not come on to her!

PEGGY. *(Voice.)* Here they come. *(Making audible grunts, Barry yanks on the drawer, lifting it up in the process. With one such pull and lift, the table topples over, scattering everything on the floor. Barry stands holding the desk drawer. He takes the briefcase and drops the drawer, reaching into his pocket for the keys to open the briefcase. They're not there. He looks at the floor, realizing he'd thrown his other keys on the desk.)*

BARRY. *(To Ashraf.)* FIND THE KEY! *(Barry starts searching the amid all the items.)* FIND IT! Oh Jesus, oh please. Don't punish me now. Wait for the weekend. *(Ashraf is halfheartedly looking around.) Get on your knees and look!*

ASHRAF. Maybe this is a sign for real.

BARRY. *(Grabbing him by the lapels.)* Listen to me: If this thing falls through I'm going to personally shove you up the dark hole from which everything you've said today has come from. Do you understand that an opportunity like this will never come your way again? *(Barry's desperation appears to seep into Ashraf, as Ashraf stares at Barry with the creeping sense that this really might be the chance of a lifetime.)*

ASHRAF. *Where did you put the key? (They both fall to the ground to search for it.)* How could you lose it? They aren't one of these? *(Holding up a set of keys on a ring.)*

BARRY. It's one key, not in a bunch.

ASHRAF. Check your pockets again. *(There's a knock on the door. Ashraf and Barry freeze.)*

BARRY. *(Whispering.)* Go out the window, get on the ledge and slip in through Peggy's office. Delay them.

ASHRAF. *(Whispering.)* It's fourteen floors.

BARRY. *(Whispering.)* It doesn't matter. You'll be dead either way if we don't open that door.

ASHRAF. *(Whispering.)* You do it.

PEGGY. *(Voice.)* Mr. Barkley?

BARRY. I'll be right there.

ASHRAF. *(Whispering.) How are we going to open the door? (Barry sees a strong-looking paperweight — or some other heavy object — and picks it up. He smashes it on the briefcase lock. The briefcase opens.)*

BARRY. *(Half-whisper.)* Yes! *(He takes out the cigar box, tries to yank it open but it won't budge. To Ashraf, less of a whisper:)* I hate you. *(The door opens. Peggy enters, followed by Cassandra Shapely and Julius Steele. The room is a mess. Ashraf and Barry are still on their knees.)*

PEGGY. *(Holding up a key.)* The, er … janitor was passing by. He had a … an extra … *(Ashraf now spots the missing key and holds that up too.)*

BARRY. *(Smiles for Peggy and company.)* Great. *(Snatches key out of Ashraf's hand.)* We were just finishing up here. You came right in the middle of the, er …

PEGGY. I was just explaining —

BARRY. Good. Come in. I'm glad you could make it. *(Barry and Ashraf stand. Barry looks particularly disheveled.)* Ms. Shapely. *(Goes to her and shakes her hand.)* Mr. Steele. *(Shakes his hand.)* Wonderful to meet you both. Thank you. We're very excited. So much so we — *(Laughs.)* went ahead and did a few scenes from the script. Hence the mess.

PEGGY. Actually I told them —

BARRY. *(Interrupting.)* You may have misunderstood. I usually lock my door when my actors want to — really feel they need to pull out all the stops. And Ashraf is one for pulling them out. Come and say hello. *(Waving Ashraf over.)* Peggy, would you mind straightening things out. *(To Julius.)* Unless you want us to leave it like this. For atmosphere? For the audition?

JULIUS. It doesn't matter. Either way.

BARRY. Either way? *(To Peggy.)* Why don't we tidy up anyway. *(Peggy starts tidying up. Introducing them.)* Ashraf. Ms. Shapely.

ASHRAF. *(Goes to shake her hand.)* Hello. Hi. *(Cassandra nods, shakes his hand.)*

BARRY. Mr. Steele.

ASHRAF. Very honored. To meet you. *(They shake hands.)*

JULIUS. I liked your Hamlet.

ASHRAF. Oh. Thank you.

JULIUS. Very impressive.

ASHRAF. Thank you.

JULIUS. I've seen some of the best take a shot at it. You definitely hold your own.

BARRY. I couldn't agree with you more.

ASHRAF. *(To Julius.)* I appreciate that.

JULIUS. I look forward to seeing what you can do with this role.

BARRY. We were just talking about the importance of theater. Can I get you anything? Soda? Coffee?

JULIUS. I would love to just get started.

BARRY. Great idea. *(Ashraf sees Peggy trying to right the table and goes over to help her.)* Never mind the — Ever helpful. I apologize again for the mess. Ashraf wanted to get a feel for the scenes and being the actor he is, really dove into it. And even drew *me* in. *(Refers to his dishevelment.)* Talk about chewing the scenery.

CASSANDRA. What scenes did you dive into?

BARRY. Excuse me? *(Cassandra picks up the* Playboy *magazine, shaking off the tissues surrounding it.)* Oh. No. That's — . No. *(To Ashraf.)* Wait: was it a visual you wanted to play against?

ASHRAF. What?

BARRY. That's right, we were talking about Kubrick. Stanley? And what is it you asked me? And I replied something about excellence in the face of vulnerability. And how the baring of the body often reveals the trembling of something luminous inside struggling to express itself?

CASSANDRA. I'm taking them to court.

BARRY. Ah.

CASSANDRA. I've requested that all copies be withdrawn from circulation.

BARRY. *(Takes magazine.)* Let's start right now. *(Holding it out to Peggy.)* Peggy? Get rid of this, please. *(Peggy will come round and take it.)*

CASSANDRA. There was an error in my prescriptions for migraines which undermined my judgement. The whole shoot was done under duress.

BARRY. That happens more often than one thinks.

CASSANDRA. I'm suing the doctor and *Playboy* for negligence and bad lighting. I consider pornography despicable and am furious I was talked into it.

BARRY. There's a shockingly fine line between art and exploitation.

CASSANDRA. There is no art about it.

BARRY. That's also a fair argument.

CASSANDRA. I wish I hadn't seen that.

BARRY. We're getting rid of it right now. *(To Peggy.)* The incinerator.

PEGGY. *(To Cassandra, clutching the magazine to her chest.)* Ms. Shapely: I so agree with you one hundred per cent. This smut *is* outrageous. It's so inspiring to me that you're taking a stand.

CASSANDRA. Thank you. Sometimes you have to stick your neck out for what you believe.

PEGGY. God yes.

CASSANDRA. I only wish I had come to my senses sooner.

PEGGY. You're doing it now.

BARRY. Peggy.

PEGGY. *(Looking at the magazine.)* And in the meantime you have nothing to be ashamed about. These are —

BARRY. *Peggy.*

PEGGY. Gorgeous.

CASSANDRA. Yes?

PEGGY. Really. They're wonderful.

CASSANDRA. You — think so?

PEGGY. Oh yes. I mean look at you. *(She's opened it to the center-fold.)* That is just such a great shot.

CASSANDRA. You don't think I … I look bloated?

PEGGY. God no. Where?

CASSANDRA. *(Pointing.)* That area.

PEGGY. The buttocks?

CASSANDRA. The lighting adds girth.

PEGGY. Not at all. I mean yes, sue them, because damn it, enough with chicks without clothes. I'm sick of passing magazine racks and having boobs jump out at me. But in the meantime, be proud of what you have.

CASSANDRA. I suppose some things survive even a bad shoot.

BARRY. That's what I meant about art shining through in spite of the exploitation. *(His interjection brings a cold end to the discussion.)* And so on. Okay, Peggy? *(Grabs a bunch of tissues from the floor, as well as the tissue box, and holds them out for Peggy to take.)* Why don't we move things along so we can start. *(Peggy takes the tissues, box and gives Barry a look, glancing down at his zipper. Barry looks at his zipper. As everyone else does in the room. He zips up his trousers. Laughing it off.)* And you thought I was kidding about Ashraf liking to pull out all the stops. *(Ashraf looks none too pleased.)* Sure we can't get you anything?

CASSANDRA. *(To Peggy.)* Bottled water would be nice.

PEGGY. Evian?

CASSANDRA. Lovely.

PEGGY. Coming right up. Mr. Steele?

JULIUS. Nothing for me.

PEGGY. I'll be right back. *(Peggy throws Barry another look before exiting.)*

BARRY. *(To Julius.)* I'll leave it to you then. Would you — like me to step out? Leave you three to — ?

JULIUS. If you have something to attend to.

BARRY. No. I can hang out in case you need anything.

JULIUS. It's up to you. This is mostly to say hello. Get to know each other. I know we're short on time. *(To Cassandra.)* When did you say you had to leave?

CASSANDRA. Soon.

JULIUS. So: this is mostly to touch base. See if we can't get something going between you and the material. Find out what we've got.

ASHRAF. Of course.

JULIUS. See how the two of you pair up, etc. Cassandra was very kind to offer her time today.

ASHRAF. *(To Cassandra.)* Thank you.

JULIUS. Cassandra will be playing Sherry. Have you read the script?

ASHRAF. Most of it. I just got it.

BARRY. He has a photographic memory. If he's read it once, he's got it down.

JULIUS. About to where?

ASHRAF. Up until the last ten pages.

JULIUS. That's fine. By then you're dead. After that it's funerals and flag-waving. Your basic swelling of emotion as the family and community reaffirm their values, etc. Do you have any questions?

BARRY. No. *(They turn to Barry.)* I mean — I don't. Ashraf might. Unless you're pressed for time.

JULIUS. If Ashraf has any questions, this would be the time to ask.

ASHRAF. Er … not right now. Maybe later on … *(Then:)* Though … I did wonder about … I was wondering about the —

BARRY. If I may suggest you ask your questions later since Ms. Shapely's on a tight schedule?

ASHRAF. Er. Okay.

JULIUS. If it's something that needs to be addressed?

BARRY. *(To Ashraf.)* I'm sorry? Is it?

ASHRAF. Not necessarily.

JULIUS. I wouldn't worry about anything on the first read.

ASHRAF. Right.

JULIUS. It's pretty straightforward. Just go with what's written.

ASHRAF. Right. *(Julius takes out a small video camera and checks it.)*

JULIUS. There's nothing too subtle or complicated about the character.

ASHRAF. Play it straight.

JULIUS. Basically.

ASHRAF. Like in: Don't signal to the audience what's going on.

JULIUS. Yes. What do you mean? *(To Barry.)* Can I use your tripod? *(Barry gets it for him.)*

ASHRAF. Be straight-faced. None of that — cheesy — winking at the audience stuff.

JULIUS. How do you mean?

ASHRAF. You know, not doing that ... not being ... *(Julius just stares at him.)* I've got you. I'm good. I know what you mean.

JULIUS. Just go with your instincts. We can get into the shadings later. For now I want to get a feel for the dynamics between the two of you. And I'd like to start with the scene where you chase Sherry into the bedroom. Her dress has been torn. She tries to lock you out but you burst in. What page is that?

CASSANDRA. *(Holding the script.)* Forty-three. *(Julius is setting up the camera. Ashraf gets the script. Cassandra slips out of her coat, revealing a provocative outfit.)*

JULIUS. Yes. So let's start there. And just go for it. We'll worry about character nuance later. Cassandra? Any questions?

CASSANDRA. I've got it.

JULIUS. If you guys could shift to that area. We'll start from there. *(They shift.)* And if you could both run in from behind the camera, and end up in that spot. *(Looking through the view-finder; to Ashraf.)* And could you take your shirt off please? I'd like to see how that looks.

ASHRAF. *(Not expecting that.)* Oh — sure. *(Julius is looking through the lens. Cassandra is shaking her arms and doing vocal warm-up exercises.)*

JULIUS. Do you have an undershirt?

ASHRAF. I do.

JULIUS. Can I see that? *(Ashraf takes off his shirt.)*
BARRY. *(Sotto voce, to Julius.)* He can always work out at the gym if you need him more pumped.
JULIUS. I don't really care.
BARRY. *(Sotto voce.)* In case. He buffs up very quickly.
JULIUS. *(To the actors.)* I might give you directions but keep going. And just mark the slaps in. Don't worry about the physical stuff. Unless the moment takes you. It's an intense, scary scene, but go for it. *(Looks through view-finder.)* Almost ready. *(Ashraf studies the script. Beat. Then looks up, ready to ask a question. He sees Barry signaling him to shut it. Julius looks up from the view-finder.)* Did you have a question?
ASHRAF. I ... No — . No. I'm sure it will become clear to me as we go on.
JULIUS. Don't be shy to ask.
ASHRAF. Well ... I was just wondering about the — how it will all ... *(Makes the coming-together sign.)* It can wait.
BARRY. I have a feeling any questions you have will instantly be clarified the moment you do the scene. Especially under Mr. Steele's expert direction.
ASHRAF. Right, right.
JULIUS. *(To Ashraf.)* Yes?
ASHRAF. Absolutely.
JULIUS. Cassandra?
CASSANDRA. Any time you're ready.
ASHRAF. Sorry.
JULIUS. Okay, so find the moment. *(Cassandra takes a deep breath.)* We are in the house of the Garner family. It's just been invaded. Every family's worst nightmare is now happening. And the biggest nightmare of all is set to occur in this scene. The phone lines are cut. You've secured the home. You're alone with the daughter. And — we're — rolling camera. *(Turns on the camera.)* Speed ... and — *(Barry gives Ashraf a thumbs-up sign.)* Action. *(Cassandra rushes in from behind the camera to the designated playing area. Ashraf follows awkwardly.)*
CASSANDRA. *(In character.)* You bastard. You bastard, stay away from me. Don't come near me. You stink. You're disgusting. You disgust me. I'd rather choke on my own vomit than kiss you. No. I won't. I won't do that. I wouldn't touch that if I was hanging off a cliff and it was the only thing left to grab. *(Slight beat. Everyone looks at Ashraf.)*
ASHRAF. I'm sorry. — I'm sorry. Can we do that again?

JULIUS. That's fine.

ASHRAF. I'm — .

JULIUS. It's okay. We'll take it again.

ASHRAF. *(Frustrated.)* Shit.

JULIUS. Not a problem. It's a tough transition. *(Cassandra walks back.)*

ASHRAF. I'm just trying to —

JULIUS. Don't worry about it. We're good. We'll take it from the top. Just relax. Take a second. Find the moment. You know what you want. She's beautiful, she's young, she's American. This is revenge *and* pleasure. *(To Cassandra.)* You know what you have to do. Honor first, self-preservation, yes, but there's also this sexual tension crackling in the air. Perverse, of course, but present in spite of yourself. And — we're rolling camera ... speed, and ... *action.* *(Cassandra runs to her spot as before. Ashraf follows after her.)*

CASSANDRA. *(In character, with more "crackle" this time.)* You bastard. You bastard, stay away from me. Don't come near me. You stink. You're disgusting. You disgust me. I'd rather choke on my own vomit than kiss you. No. I won't. I won't do that. I wouldn't touch that if I was dangling off a cliff and it was the only thing left to grab. No! *(Ashraf freezes again. Slight beat.)*

ASHRAF. Shit. I — . *Damn.*

JULIUS. Relax.

ASHRAF. I — . Shit.

JULIUS. What is it?

ASHRAF. I — don't know what's — I'm ... there's —

CASSANDRA. Honey? If I intimidate you, just remember: At the end of the day, I'm just another struggling actor like you.

ASHRAF. That's not it.

CASSANDRA. Oh. Then get over it. We don't have all day.

ASHRAF. I'm just trying to — I can't seem to get a lock on the ...

JULIUS. You're thinking too much about it. Don't overthink it.

ASHRAF. If I could just plug into the ... 'Cause it's — . The tone is so — . I understand that's the point. That it's so over the top that it signals the break with reality we need in order to understand where we are.

BARRY. Ashraf.

ASHRAF. But on one level it seems so — dead serious. And kind of undermines that great edge that runs through it. So I'm wondering, how do I as a — full-fledged character inhabit a cardboard cartoon functioning in a, you know, satire. And it's not like I haven't done satire before, but there's something about the tone in this one that keeps — tripping me up, you know. I can't quite get my mind around what end of funny this man is coming from.

JULIUS. What satire?

ASHRAF. Er. This one? *(Clarifying.)* This, er — the one we're — . This one.

JULIUS. This script?

ASHRAF. Yes?

JULIUS. You think it's a satire?

ASHRAF. Er — yes?

JULIUS. Is that your reading?

ASHRAF. It's not?

JULIUS. Not last I checked.

ASHRAF. Ah.

JULIUS. A strange thing to say. What made you think that?

ASHRAF. Nothing. — Actually. I didn't. — That's what I thought too. — That it wasn't.

JULIUS. I hope not. We're in trouble if it is.

ASHRAF. Right.

JULIUS. Is this — is this something we need to address?

ASHRAF. No. Not at all. — No. I was thinking there was a — like a — back door into this when — in fact — there is no other way in than the one that is plainly in sight. There it is. In black and white. In fact: *(A laugh of sorts.)* It is black and white.

JULIUS. Pretty much.

ASHRAF. It is what it is. And was all the time.

JULIUS. That's its strength.

ASHRAF. That's why it packs a wallop.

JULIUS. That's what we hope to deliver.

ASHRAF. And I'm here to deliver it.

JULIUS. I'd certainly like to count on you. I saw something in your Hamlet that I think would bring a much needed element to this part.

ASHRAF. You saw a connection between Hamlet and *this* guy?

JULIUS. Between you and the gravity you bring to your roles. I have every confidence you can make something of this character. Fill it out. Make it real. Would you do that for us? I would be honored to have you be a part of this.

CASSANDRA. *(Under her breath.)* And I thought I was high maintenance.

ASHRAF. I'm … really flattered that you would want me. It's not every day you get asked by Julius Steele to be in a film of his. Opposite Cassandra Shapely, for God's sakes. I would have to be nuts not to want to be a part of this. I mean — how insane would you have to be to say no.

BARRY. Pretty insane.

JULIUS. Is there something the matter?

ASHRAF. So: — This is the film you're going to make?

JULIUS. We certainly hope we can do it justice. What is it, Ashraf? It feels like you want to say something.

ASHRAF. No … Except … *(Slight beat.)* I hope I can do it justice too.

JULIUS. Then we're on the same page, because I very much want to.

ASHRAF. Then damn it … I'd better get my act together. *(A laugh of sorts.)*

BARRY. *(Laughs.)* Yes.

ASHRAF. You know … can I just get one thing from my bag that I think will help?

JULIUS. Make it quick, we've got to move this along. *(To Cassandra.)* Sorry, Cass; thanks for hanging in there.

BARRY. Thoroughbred racehorse nervous at the gate.

CASSANDRA. *(Sotto voce, to Julius.)* He better be worth it.

JULIUS. *(To Barry.)* I hope so too. *(During the above exchange, Ashraf has gone to his bag and taken out a small handgun.)*

ASHRAF. Is it okay if I use this?

BARRY. OhmyGod.

ASHRAF. Something tangible to ground me.

JULIUS. Is that a prop?

ASHRAF. I don't think it's the prop one. My neighborhood is kinda dicey. But it's not loaded. *(Checking.)* Is it?

JULIUS. I don't know that we need it.

ASHRAF. The safety's on and it's rusted out. I don't think it would fire no matter how many times you pulled the trigger. *(Points it at Barry, who ducks.)*

BARRY. *(Alarmed.)* No.

ASHRAF. It's just to scare people off. I'll keep it tucked in my belt.

JULIUS. I'd feel safer if you didn't.

ASHRAF. Sure? To bolster the scene? — Alright, no matter. *(Throws the gun back into the bag as he reaches to get something else.)* How about this? *(He takes out a keffiyeh.)*

JULIUS. Good. Yes.

ASHRAF. *(Wraps it around himself.)* Probably more appropriate for the mood. I never leave home without it. What faster way to say "*outré*," or "watch out," than having a keffiyeh around. Who says fashion doesn't pack a punch.

JULIUS. *(Seeing the result.)* Yes, good, that'll work.

ASHRAF. Sure about the gun?

JULIUS. Perhaps later.

ASHRAF. And how about an accent?

JULIUS. What?

ASHRAF. A Middle Eastern accent?

JULIUS. Well he's not from the Ukraine is he.

BARRY. *(A nervous laugh.)* "He's not from the Ukraine."

ASHRAF. No. He's not. One accent coming up.

JULIUS. Okay. So take a moment. And this time why don't we start from that spot already, and just give us your last line. *(They move into place.)* So take a moment. Deep breaths. Remember where we are. Mohammed and the others have just tied the family up. They've helped themselves to the dinner. His hands are all greasy, if you will, if you want to focus on something tactile, to ground yourself. Also, smell. Smell is important. She talks about him smelling, what does that mean? He's dragged Sherry away from her family. She's broken loose and run into the bedroom. He chases her. She tries to lock it, he breaks in. And — full throttle. Roll camera, sound, and — action. *(Cassandra runs in panting, followed by Ashraf.)*

CASSANDRA. *(In character.)* No! Don't come near me. I'll — *(Gasps.)* Oh God no.

ASHRAF. *(In character.)* It is only handkerchief I take out. You have gravy on mouth. I wipe it off.

CASSANDRA. *(In character.)* Stay away from me.

JULIUS. Mohammed has unbuckled his belt. Just mark it in. *(Ashraf unbuckles his belt.)* Unless you —

ASHRAF. *(In character.)* I keep it in safe place where I not lose it.

CASSANDRA. *(In character.)* I'd rather kill myself.

ASHRAF. *(In character.)* Oops: no handkerchief, but look what I have instead.

CASSANDRA. *(In character.)* Why are you doing this? What have we ever done to you?

ASHRAF. *(In character.)* Nothing yet. But we change that.

CASSANDRA. *(In character.)* Get away from me.

ASHRAF. *(In character.)* Now you taste hummus. Better than gravy and stuffing.

CASSANDRA. *(In character.)* I'll kill myself.

JULIUS. She picks up a letter opener from the desk.

CASSANDRA. *(In character.)* I will. Don't come near me.

JULIUS. She places the point against her throat.

ASHRAF. *(In character.)* Let me see precious blood.

CASSANDRA. *(In character.)* I'll do it.

ASHRAF. *(In character.)* I have you either way.

CASSANDRA. *(In character.)* You *bastard.*

JULIUS. She lunges with the letter opener. *(Cassandra moves to stab him.)* He knocks it away. *(Ashraf knocks it out of her hand.)* Slaps her. *(Ashraf mimes slapping her twice, once across each cheek. Each time Cassandra jerks her head to the side.)* Good. And she collapses. *(Cassandra falls.)*

CASSANDRA. *(In character, in tears.)* God will punish you for this.

ASHRAF. *(In character.)* Do not speak of God. You are all Godless. Get on bed.

CASSANDRA. *(In character.)* Please. I beg you. I made a promise to my fiancé. Can't you respect that?

ASHRAF. *(In character.)* We phone him; tell him what happens.

CASSANDRA. *(In character.)* I've read about your culture. It's big on modesty for women. I respect you for that. Show me the same courtesy.

ASHRAF. *(In character.)* I am big for women too. Want to see how big?

CASSANDRA. *(In character. Gets up at this point.)* You pig. Open your eyes. I am a human being too. Treat me as one.

ASHRAF. *(In character.)* Okay. I compromise. I take your ass instead.

CASSANDRA. *(In character.)* No!

ASHRAF. *(In character.)* I help you out. I do not take virginity.

CASSANDRA. *(In character.)* *That's not a compromise.*

ASHRAF. *(In character.)* Where I come from it is.

CASSANDRA. *(In character.)* Have you no concept of *hygiene,* you *idiot*?

ASHRAF. *(In character.)* You call me idiot?

CASSANDRA. *(In character.)* Well you're not showing signs of intelligence are you.

ASHRAF. *(In character, grabs her, pulls her in close.)* Enough with mouth. Get on bed.

CASSANDRA. *(In character.)* Wait a minute! Wait. Don't you want me to be nice for you? Freshen up?

ASHRAF. *(In character.)* You fresh now.

CASSANDRA. *(In character.)* I want to put lipstick on for you. Be really pretty.

ASHRAF. *(In character.)* You pretty now.

CASSANDRA. *(In character.)* I haven't brushed my teeth or anything.

ASHRAF. *(In character.)* Forget teeth.

CASSANDRA. *(In character.)* I can't! Don't you want me to love you back? I'm too self-conscious going into it like this.

ASHRAF. *(In character.)* Tough. We do it now.

CASSANDRA. *(In character.)* Allow me a shred of dignity, for chrissakes!

ASHRAF. *(In character, slight beat.)* Okay. Put lipstick. But hurry, I have hostages waiting.

CASSANDRA. *(In character.)* Thank you. It'll make all the difference. You'll see.

JULIUS. She turns around to the dresser, picks up the hair brush.

CASSANDRA. *(In character.)* I know the women where you come from are so feminine. I don't want to be any less in your eyes. Even though this is a criminal act *and* a rape, let's not forget *that*. Still: there's no reason why we can't make-believe and pretend it's not.

JULIUS. She puts on the lipstick.

CASSANDRA. *(In character.)* Create a little magic for ourselves. In the midst of all this *horror*. I want it to be just right. If this is going to be the day, there's no reason why I can't block everything out and pretend you're someone else.

ASHRAF. *(In character.)* I make you feel good. *(Ashraf grabs her by the waist.)*

CASSANDRA. *(In character.)* Wait. I'm almost done. I want it to be just perfect, just right. So the last thing you see —

JULIUS. And she's grabbed the scissors.

CASSANDRA. *(In character, turning around.)* Is my pretty face sending you to *hell*.

JULIUS. And she — *(Cassandra raises her arm to plunge the imaginary scissors into his chest. The door opens and Peggy enters with the bottled water. All heads turn to Peggy. She holds out the bottled water. Everyone remains frozen for a second. Peggy exits, closing door behind her.)* She plunges the scissors into his chest.

CASSANDRA. *(In character.)* Die, die, die! ... Die! *(Each "die" accompanied with a plunging of the imaginary scissors. Cassandra in character stares at him, horrified at what she's done. Ashraf in character stares at her with a sardonic smile. Ashraf grabs the "embedded scissors" from the area near his collarbone and yanks it out. And throws it down. He also throws the script away.)*

ASHRAF. *(In character.)* You make me like you more.

CASSANDRA. *(In character.)* I don't care what you do with me. But don't hurt my family. I beg of you.

ASHRAF. *(In character.)* You Americans. You make us bleed. And then you ask us to be nice.

CASSANDRA. *(In character.)* We haven't done anything to you. We're innocent.

ASHRAF. *(In character.)* What you call this? *(Referring to the wound.)* A love bite?

CASSANDRA. *(In character.)* I'm defending myself.

ASHRAF. *(In character.)* I do same. *(He grabs her by the waist and pulls her in close.)* I take you before you take us.

CASSANDRA. *(In character.)* No. Jesus. Your breath stinks.

ASHRAF. *(In character.)* Good. I bring you back garbage you make us eat. Now I make you eat it. You taste what we taste. My kiss is kiss of thousands you kill. I bring them back from dead.

CASSANDRA. *(In character.)* No. Have pity.

ASHRAF. *(In character.)* Later I have pity. Tonight I have you. *(Ashraf draws her in even closer.)*

CASSANDRA. *(In character.)* Ugh! *(Ashraf boldly kisses her. They break but he still holds onto her.)*

ASHRAF. *(In character.)* Excuse me: I bleed on pretty dress.

CASSANDRA. *(In character, slightly breathless from the kiss.)* You're a monster.

ASHRAF. *(In character.)* Take off dress. We take it to dry cleaners. *(Cassandra pushes away from him, throws her script down.)*

CASSANDRA. *(In character.)* No.

ASHRAF. *(In character.)* Tonight you become woman.

CASSANDRA. *(In character.)* Never. I'd rather be buried alive. *(Ashraf kisses her again.)*

JULIUS. Good ... good ... and ... cut. *(The actors break.)* Good. Yes.

BARRY. Wow.

JULIUS. Good. Excellent.

BARRY. Wow.

JULIUS. You did great. Very powerful stuff.

CASSANDRA. *(A flirtatious smile.)* He wasn't bad. Not bad at all. *(Cassandra goes to her bag to get a cigarette.)*

JULIUS. All that psyching up was worth it after all

BARRY. You blew me away. You both did. Wow.

JULIUS. You took it where it needed to go. Just the right level of menace. *(To Cassandra.)* Did that come across from your end?

CASSANDRA. *(Flirtatious.)* Among other things.

JULIUS. There's definitely a chemistry worth exploring there. That was a question you helped answer today.

BARRY. *(Patting Ashraf.)* My boy here brings good chemistry to any project he's in. Always does. *(Barry goes to light Cassandra's cigarette. Note: If the actor doesn't want to smoke the cigarette, then Cassandra can just wave the offered light away. It could also be one of those fake cigarettes.)*

JULIUS. You brought a level of realness that other actors would simply miss. The swagger, the focus. In fact … *(To Cassandra.)* I'm inspired enough to try out another scene. Cass? Five more minutes? I'll have you out before lunch.

CASSANDRA. *(Looks at her watch.)* Sure. Why not. Might as well think of this as a rehearsal. *(To Barry.)* Can you let her in; I'm parched.

BARRY. Will do. *(Barry goes to open the door.)*

JULIUS. *(Moves camera for another set-up.)* The scene's on page sixty-five, where Sherry has made the switch and starts defending Mohammed in front of her family. Mohammed is flipping the TV channels and egging her on. At this point, I believe, Mohammed is walking around in his shorts. *(To Ashraf.)* If you wouldn't mind. *(Barry has opened the door over the above speech and lets Peggy in. Ashraf stands there, not sure he's understood the request. Barry signals for him to remove his trousers, mouthing the word "off." Ashraf mechanically takes them off. Cassandra speaks over this.)*

CASSANDRA. I'm thinking she wouldn't be wearing a whole lot herself at this point. Which I think would convey how far she's traveled from her Christian summer camp mentality to this post-sex moment.

JULIUS. What are you thinking?

CASSANDRA. Tank top. No bra. Maybe an article of his clothing to show that symbiotic thing that's developing between them.

JULIUS. You want to try that now?

CASSANDRA. Might as well.

JULIUS. Let's do it.

PEGGY. I'm sorry for barging in. I had to run across the street.

But: I have to say: I couldn't help overhearing the scene and I must tell you it was — *amazing*. Oh my God.

CASSANDRA. Thanks. Could you help me unclasp this? *(Peggy hands her the water as she starts to unclasp the bra.)*

PEGGY. If it was that good just hearing it, it's going to be awesome. You so rock Ms. Shapely.

CASSANDRA. Thank you. Hold these? *(Cassandra hands Peggy the water and cigarette as she reaches under her clothing to remove the bra.)*

PEGGY. Just when you think you know how it's done, someone comes along and shows you no, this is how it's really done. It's just so astonishing to me how actors become other people at the drop of a hat. I can barely lie without going red in the face.

CASSANDRA. Exchange. *(She hands Peggy the bra as she takes back the cigarette and water.)*

PEGGY. *(Moved.)* That is so nice of you.

CASSANDRA. No. I meant: Can you put it with my stuff over there.

PEGGY. Oh.

CASSANDRA. Besides, I think we're different cup sizes.

PEGGY. Of course.

CASSANDRA. Unless you really want it.

PEGGY. Can I?

BARRY. Peggy. *(Peggy defensively mouths the words, "I'll just hold onto it," to Barry.)*

CASSANDRA. *(To Ashraf.)* Mind if I use your undershirt for a tank top? I imagine she'd choose that to wear. Something he's sweated in. *(Ashraf looks at her. Then takes off his undershirt and hands it to her. She takes it flirtatiously.)* I hope I haven't left you in the cold.

ASHRAF. No.

CASSANDRA. You know … you have naturally even goosebumps. They'll blow up well on screen. Trust me, it makes a difference. Careers have been made on it. *(To Peggy.)* Hon. Mind if I use you for a shield while I change into this.

PEGGY. Thank you. *(They go off into a corner. Ashraf turns to Julius, ready to ask him a question but is interrupted by:)*

BARRY. *(Sotto voce, to Ashraf.)* Socks. Take them off. They look stupid. And gym, lots of gym.

JULIUS. *(To Barry.)* Could we move those chairs to the corner there and imagine that as the TV area.

BARRY. Done. Ashraf? Could you help?

ASHRAF. No. *(To Julius.)* So. This isn't then — . This is definitely not — *not* a satire.

JULIUS. *(Busy with the new set-up.)* Are we still on that?

BARRY. *(To Ashraf.)* Could I get some help here.

JULIUS. I find satires reductive and mean-spirited. I'm not sure the genre helps you explore anything. Least of all something as important as the threat to a family and its values. I'm curious where you got that idea?

ASHRAF. So ... what genre would you say this is then?

BARRY. *Ashraf?*

JULIUS. I'd like to think of it as a psychological drama. With a good deal of action thrown in to please the producers.

ASHRAF. Psychological drama?

JULIUS. If I do my job right, yes. And with the actors I have giving the kind of performances I just saw.

ASHRAF. But — what I just gave you was dreck.

JULIUS. Well. You don't have to be modest about it.

ASHRAF. No no: It was dreck.

JULIUS. There's no need to be modest around me.

ASHRAF. I'm not.

BARRY. He's exceptionally modest.

ASHRAF. You don't understand, I was *trying* to be awful. The only thing stinking out there wasn't Mohammed's breath, it was the work I just turned in. I was purposely trying to be lousy. You could squeeze more psychology out of a lemon than from what I just did.

JULIUS. It's odd to me how the people who give you the best work are usually the ones most hard on themselves. Or maybe that's the reason.

BARRY. The talent suffers to bring forth the fruits we enjoy. Look at Van Gogh.

JULIUS. I'm not sure you have to suffer.

BARRY. My boy's complicated but he delivers.

ASHRAF. *(To Julius.)* Are you saying you actually liked, genuinely liked what I just did and weren't just thinking, "Well, at least we have someone from the right ethnic group playing this"?

CASSANDRA. *(Looking in the hand-mirror Peggy is holding.)* Do I hear someone fishing for more compliments? You're worse than me. You're going to have to negotiate the size of this man's trailer up front.

BARRY. *(A nervous laugh.)* I'm on it. And maybe throw in a new therapist.

ASHRAF. But — I'm not joking. What I just gave you was crap. It was unmitigated ka-ka. With special focus on making execrable choices in case I was being too subtle.

JULIUS. Well your character isn't subtle is he.

ASHRAF. Not subtle? He isn't there. I wasn't inhabiting anything. He's a string of clichés hung together with punctuation marks. I could find more life reading a Denny's menu. At least there's the promise of something more meaty in a Denny's menu.

BARRY. Could you help me set up the scene, please, now, Ashraf? Right now.

ASHRAF. Are you really going ahead with this? As is?

BARRY. Ashraf.

ASHRAF. This crap? With this crappy character? Surrounded by his gang of equally evil, crappy characters in a lousy set-up with a shitty ending that leaves you feeling like you've been sucking on a sewer for a hundred-twenty pages? *(At some point Julius has stopped what he's doing to focus on Ashraf.)*

JULIUS. I'm not sure I'm understanding this. Is this a process you go through as an actor? Breaking something down so you can build it up again and make it your own? Or are you saying you don't like the script?

BARRY. Very much the former.

ASHRAF. Mr. Steele: You can't do this. You of all people. You look out for people. You champion causes. If you're the moral compass in this business, then we're screwed. You've got to know what this is.

JULIUS. So you *don't* like the script.

BARRY. On the contrary, it's his way of digesting the material, he always does this.

ASHRAF. *(Ignoring Barry.)* Maybe you misread it. It happens. You're juggling a hundred things and were probably distracted and thought it was something it wasn't.

BARRY. I really don't think it's for you to be so presumptuous as to assume anything of the kind.

JULIUS. What is it that you don't like exactly?

ASHRAF. *How could you not see it?*

BARRY. Because not everyone sees a slight in every remark. *(To Julius.)* He's sensitive, but that's why he's good.

JULIUS. I'd like to know what offends you about it.

ASHRAF. You really don't see it?

JULIUS. I want to get your take on it, never mind what I think.

BARRY. Why? These are very personal issues that don't really have any bearing on the matter at hand.

ASHRAF. *(To Barry.)* Fraudulent crap that solidifies drivel so that people go around thinking the worse of others, that's not relevant?

BARRY. *It's a movie.*

ASHRAF. And you're a dick, Barry.

JULIUS. Whoa, whoa, let's calm this down. You feel people are being misrepresented in this movie?

ASHRAF. Why am I the only one who sees this? *(Barry is about to respond but Julius holds up his hand.)* The pages groan with it. There are enough stereotypes here to create a whole new cartoon network.

CASSANDRA. Stereotypes?

ASHRAF. Even the family comes off as idiots. *(To Cassandra.)* And your character: it's like she's been ripped out of a Norman Rockwell painting and thrown into some atrocious "B" movie that progressively gets worse.

CASSANDRA. You don't like what I just did?

ASHRAF. *What you're being forced to play.*

CASSANDRA. I'm not forced to do anything. That performance was given of my own free will.

JULIUS. You think it's full of stereotypes?

ASHRAF. Please don't say that like I've gone mad. You've got to see that. This movie is the equivalent of me picking up this gun *(Picks up the gun.)* and threatening everyone in this room.

BARRY. Oh God, meltdown.

ASHRAF. That's how deadly this stuff is in the long run. It blows a hole in the minds of the audience until they actually think this garbage is true. That people of my ethnic persuasion are naturally violent and prone to blow up at the slightest thing. That we're vicious and a menace to decent people everywhere.

BARRY. Ashraf.

ASHRAF. *(Pointing the gun at Barry.)* And that's just not so, you prick.

BARRY. I believe you.

ASHRAF. No you don't. That's why you showed me this script, and why it's going to get made.

JULIUS. We'd feel a lot more comfortable if you put that gun down.

ASHRAF. You see: I pick up a gun and it's threatening. Other people might pick up a gun and you'd understand they were trying to make a point.

JULIUS. We get your point.

ASHRAF. No you don't. Look: the proof is in the pudding, you feel threatened. With somebody else you'd look beyond the gun and hear what he's saying.

BARRY. Any actor who's hysterical and has a gun is threatening regardless of his ethnic persuasion.

ASHRAF. *(Points the gun at Barry.)* Don't tempt me, Barry. Don't fricckin' tempt me.

BARRY. Oh grow up and stop being such a dumbass. If that gun wasn't loaded and I wasn't sufficiently intimidated by a real gun in the hands of a hysteric, I'd come over there and slap some sense into you.

ASHRAF. You know what, Barry, you're fired.

BARRY. Eat my dick.

ASHRAF. No, you taste my hummus, you fuck.

BARRY. No, *you* fuck, you ass.

ASHRAF. Fuck you.

JULIUS. Excuse me. *(Ashraf swings around and inadvertently points the gun at Julius.)* Easy there.

ASHRAF. Please: Don't make this movie. You don't have to; you don't need it. Why are you making this movie?

JULIUS. Why don't we talk about it.

ASHRAF. Promise me you won't make it.

JULIUS. Alright, let's talk about it.

ASHRAF. Don't talk to me like I've lost it. I've not lost it! *(To Barry.)* Get away from that door.

BARRY. Are you holding us hostage? Jesus God, we're hostages.

ASHRAF. Everybody. Would you all calm down. I'm not threatening anyone. You're only making my point by thinking the worse. Which only pisses me off more and makes me want to threaten somebody for real.

CASSANDRA. *(To Ashraf.)* Hey! *(Ashraf swings around to Cassandra, inadvertently pointing the gun at her. Peggy throws her body in front of Cassandra.)* That's sweet of you, hon. Why don't you get me another cigarette. It's in my bag. *(Still feeling protective, Peggy complies.)* Pardon me if I'm missing the point here, but maybe I'm slow. Let me understand this: You're pissed off because in this script — you see your character as getting the short end of the stick? As far as not being warm and cuddly and acting like a stereotype?

ASHRAF. I'd settle for a stereotype. At least that implies something two-dimensional. This is a monotype. Not even a type. There's no such creature in the natural world that corresponds to my character. He's a bad joke with real-world consequences.

CASSANDRA. You don't like it in other words.

ASHRAF. No.

CASSANDRA. And you've never done a major movie before?

ASHRAF. No.

CASSANDRA. You're a theater rat.

ASHRAF. What has that got to do with anything?

CASSANDRA. A theater rat who's being given a big break.

ASHRAF. This can't be my big break, it would be too awful.

CASSANDRA. Listen to me you whimpering little gas bag. Let me tell you something about playing crap for a living. Are you listening? Because I'm only going to say this once before I leave you all to jack off about whatever it is you want to jack off about. *(Peggy gives her a lit cigarette. Note: it could also be unlit.)* Thanks.

PEGGY. Tell it like it is.

CASSANDRA. You're a doll.

PEGGY. I've got your back.

CASSANDRA. *(To Ashraf.)* So you're miffed you're not playing a boffo character with a great personality and charm to spare. Well, boo-hoo, my pussy weeps for you. Excuse me while I break out the tissues for another struggling actor asked to play shit and make it real. What the hell kind of business do you think this is? An academy for the study of human behavior? This is the land of gummybears and popcorn, and making out in the back row and leaving a mess for the ushers to clean up. It ain't deep; it's not real, and if you're lucky you get paid a whole lot. *(Ashraf opens his mouth to say something but she holds her hand up)* Pfft. Shove it. I don't want to hear it. Save it for after I leave. Do you think I got to where I am today because I was picky. I'm *a woman*. Do you know what I get offered as *a* woman? In a business that prizes eye-candy before everything else? Boobs and ass before character and content? Honey: the pickings are slim. I get my choice of whores, skanks, saints, or virgins. And that's when I'm not being offered whores, skanks, saints, or virgins. Or bitches. Or warrior princesses with penis envy. Or any combination of the above. The trough is full of swill, hon, and always has been, and if you're lucky you find one or two great nuggets in your career and that's what you live off while you forage through more trash. Stereotypes, please. You don't know anything about stereotypes until you've walked in my hooker boots for six weeks on a movie set. Get over it.

I know my part isn't great. But I'm going to give it everything I have and make those pimply kids in the back row stop tonguing for two minutes and give me their full sex-crazed attention because goddamn it I deserve it. And if you've got any balls, you'll take this part and do the same. You're an actor. Act like one you little piss-ant. *(She picks up her bag and clothes.)* You all think on that while I go make some calls. And when I get back, if you're not finished agonizing over whatever it is you've got your boxers in a twist about, then — I'm gone.

PEGGY. *(Offering to carry her stuff.)* I've got it.

CASSANDRA. Thanks. I'm looking for an assistant, you know.

PEGGY. I'm available.

CASSANDRA. You're hired. *(Cassandra moves to the door.)* Sorry, Julius. But I don't have time for this. Good luck. *(She exits.)*

PEGGY. *(To Ashraf.)* You should be ashamed of yourself. You are such a spaz. *(Peggy exits.)*

JULIUS. *(To Barry.)* Perhaps you'd better leave us alone as well.

BARRY. I don't know where to begin —

JULIUS. *(Interrupting.)* It's okay. We won't be too long. *(Sees Barry's concern.)* I'll be okay. *(Barry gives Ashraf another look, then exits, closing the door behind him. Slight beat.)*

ASHRAF. Oh God. Look at me. How did I get here? I'm not this.

JULIUS. I'm sure you're not.

ASHRAF. I'm not. I'm a wonderful worker who works well with others and never complains. Or uses a gun. Even when I disagree with someone.

JULIUS. I don't mind, as long you promise to use that same passion for the role.

ASHRAF. I'm not a gun-toting fanatic, even if I'm behaving like one.

JULIUS. Well you do want to be careful: fanatics usually start off with a reasonable premise.

ASHRAF. Then you *do* think I have a reasonable premise.

JULIUS. It would be more reasonable if you put that gun away.

ASHRAF. This? It's not loaded. It's not even real. It's a keepsake from a murder-mystery I did last summer. Look. *(He fires it in the air. A loud bang.)* Wrong gun. *(Ashraf drops the gun. The door flies open. Barry, Cassandra, and Peggy appear.)*

JULIUS. We're fine. Ashraf was just showing me what he wasn't. *(To Cassandra.)* Make your calls. I'll be with you in a sec. *(The others look concerned.)* I'm fine, really. We'll be done in five. *(Cassandra, now back in her own shirt, tosses Ashraf's undershirt into the room. Julius closes the door. Ashraf collapses into a chair. At some point during the exchange below, Ashraf will put his clothes back on.)*

ASHRAF. I should shoot myself. I'm dead. I'll never work in this town again. Word will get out that I'm insane.

JULIUS. Not necessarily. Though Cassandra does have a point.

ASHRAF. I'd settle for saints and virgins. Even warrior princesses with penis envy. That would feel like a real breakthrough.

JULIUS. You're making too much of it.

ASHRAF. How can you say that when you've been so careful handling other causes and groups.

JULIUS. I don't handle causes. I handle a camera. I make movies.

ASHRAF. You care about the subjects you make movies about, I know you do.

JULIUS. Insofar as my subjects tell a good story.

ASHRAF. This is a good story?

JULIUS. I believe it is, yes.

ASHRAF. How? Unless this has become like so much white noise you don't see it. Or it's some reverse PC to show no one's beholden to anyone's agenda?

JULIUS. Give me specifics so we can address your concerns.

ASHRAF. Don't you see why I'm frothing at the mouth? The very question is offensive.

JULIUS. I can't help you if you won't show me what upsets you?

ASHRAF. Pick a page. Any page. Let's see. Here's one. A real gem: *(Reading.)* "Allah be praised. You have great tits. They are like dates. They remind me of home."

JULIUS. How would you change that?

ASHRAF. Burn the script. That would solve it.

JULIUS. How would you adjust the line?

ASHRAF. Kill the writer.

JULIUS. Ashraf.

ASHRAF. I'm serious. That would be the perfect rewrite.

JULIUS. Work with me here.

ASHRAF. For starters, what's with this "Allah"? Every time writers want to get ethnic on an Arab they throw in "Allah," like that's a character trait — no, a character fault that immediately tells you the guy is a loony. 'Cause only loonies say "Allah" just before they do something violent. And it's not "Allah," it's "God." They're not separate gods. It's the same God. So just say "God." As in, "God be praised, the writer's a jerk and should be killed."

JULIUS. Done. We'll change it to "God." What else?

ASHRAF. But that's cosmetic.

JULIUS. How about the rest of the line? It's okay?

ASHRAF. No, it's trash. "Like dates"?

JULIUS. Another fruit? Less offensive?

ASHRAF. It's not about the fruit.

JULIUS. Less specifically local. Oranges?

ASHRAF. No fruits at all.

JULIUS. "God be praised, you have great tits," leave it at that?

ASHRAF. Would he really say "tits."

JULIUS. Breasts?

ASHRAF. Forget breasts, it's tacky, whatever you call them. And "They remind me of home"?

JULIUS. Cut that too?

ASHRAF. Cut everything.

JULIUS. Then why don't we just make it a reaction shot. He sees her, he's aroused, we cut to his face. We avoid the line. And any other lines you don't like, we'll look at them. Whatever makes you more comfortable.

ASHRAF. Really? — You still want me after all this?

JULIUS. I see something that could work. If you'll just let it. *(Slight beat.)*

ASHRAF. But why does it have to be this film? Why isn't my dream director asking me to do another film? Like a romantic comedy. A visiting Arab dignitary discovers the joys of windsurfing when he visits Hawaii and falls for the scuba-diving instructor. And then has to persuade his parents that a life on the beach won't undermine his religious obligations. Or, or an action sci-fi where a muscled Arab American in a Marine uniform fights off a horde of creepy aliens who've come to suck our bone marrow because that's like oil in their world. And there's a showdown in the mosque. Or, okay, maybe the mosque thing is too much and he doesn't have to be a Muslim but: — *You don't make films with villains. Why are you starting now?*

JULIUS. You know … my great-grandfather was Polish, back when the terrorists were anarchists, and the papers were screaming about foreigners. Poles and Italians were being rounded up and kicked out of the country. Around every corner there was supposed to be a terrorist waiting to hurl a bomb at you.

ASHRAF. *Right.* Would you have made a film about a Polish terrorist back then? *No.*

JULIUS. I would have jumped at the chance.

ASHRAF. No you would not.

JULIUS. Sure I would. And miss out on a hot story?

ASHRAF. And inflame the situation by catering to everyone's prejudice?

JULIUS. It's not a prejudice when it's real. There *were* Polish anarchists. It's the exceptional that makes the story. It's man-bites-dog. That's why people pay attention.

ASHRAF. But don't you feel a sense of responsibility?

JULIUS. To telling a good story, yes. You want to do morality, become a preacher, or write a book.

ASHRAF. I don't believe I'm hearing this. What about your other films?

JULIUS. Did you ever feel you were being hit over the head with something?

ASHRAF. *No*, there was subtlety, ambiguity. Everything this film is missing.

JULIUS. As well as clearly defined characters in simple stories.

ASHRAF. With no villains.

JULIUS. There *were* villains.

ASHRAF. Not a whole group like here.

JULIUS. Where is that stated in the script? I wouldn't have touched it if it was.

ASHRAF. Oh come on, you know how it works. It's the poop splash effect. We all get tarnished. One poisonous image at a time.

JULIUS. You're on a mission for serious control here.

ASHRAF. I'm just asking for some acknowledgement that I'm not talking out of my behind.

JULIUS. And your solution is what? Censorship? (*Interrupts Ashraf before he can reply.*) I *know* it's not all there. You should have seen the state some of my earlier films started out in. It will be a very different script by the time we roll.

ASHRAF. It would have to be unrecognizable to this. — This is so depressing. I feel like I'm meeting my god and he's not understanding a word I'm saying.

JULIUS. Ashraf. Look. I'm not stupid. I know there are bad feelings out there now. Focused on a group of people, a religion, yours, but that will pass. It always does. It's an old tradition of this country that all newcomers pass through this gauntlet of negative crap before being accepted into the fold. It's like a reverse welcome mat. The latest outsiders carry the burden that was carried by the strangers that came before them. Suspicion rules. Do you know Carl Jung? Projecting shadows? He gets into that; you should read him. My advice? Don't run from it. Don't stand on the side and lob rocks. Get in this film and shake it up. Within limits, of course. We don't have the luxury of these discussions when we start rolling. But do it. Risk it. The more you do, the lighter the load gets for those that follow. I mean look at what we're doing: we're changing the script even now. But Ashraf, you have to jump in. You have to commit.

ASHRAF. Can I ask you one last question? What do you really see in this script? What kind of film could you possibly make from this story?

JULIUS. *(Shrugs.)* It's primal. A family under siege. Trying to survive. Who couldn't identify with that? Even you and your family. You can't get more visceral. *(He goes to retrieve his camera.)* Take a few minutes. Think on what we talked about while I go check on Cassandra. We will need an answer before we leave. I hope it's a yes. *(Shakes his hand.)* It was good meeting you. Maybe I'll see you again. *(Julius smiles, opens the door, and exits. Ashraf looks shell-shocked. Slight beat. Barry enters, closes the door. Slight beat.)*

BARRY. Cantwell's out there … Groveling … Before Cassandra … It's always instructive to see your boss begging. It puts a perspective on how much more you have to learn on ways to debase yourself to get what you want. — He wants to kill you … I've asked him to hold off on that. As your agent, I feel I should have first crack at that. Then, if you're still breathing, I think you should be passed around the office and systematically get beaten up by everyone whose job you may have imperiled. But the strange thing is … Julius still wants you. *(A disbelieving laugh.)* He waits for your answer. Imagine. He's off to lunch. Wants to know what you've decided after he's done. Established stars have suffered for doing less, but he, the great Julius, is waiting on you. A nobody. — A less than nobody. — A fart. That some drama school blew out of its curriculum. Less than a fart. A know-nothing stink. A cretin. A retarded know-nothing stink cretin with the brain capacity of a piece of chewed-up bubble gum spat into the toilet and flushed out to sea where all other washed-out, talentless non-starters wash up and die and get buried in little sand-castles where bratty little kids with no bladder control play. *(Slight beat.)* I love you, you know that … You're like my own — *(Taps his heart.*) in a weird, non-sexual sort of way. (*Slight beat. He gets on his knees before Ashraf.*) Please. For God's sake. Come to your senses. (*Throws his arms around Ashraf.*) Ashraf. Say yes. Just say yes. That's all you have to do.

ASHRAF. Barry.

BARRY. Say it.

ASHRAF. Let go.

BARRY. Just say it.

ASHRAF. Let go, Barry.

BARRY. I'll do anything. What do you want? You want to slap me, slap me. I deserve it. I'm a bad man, I really am. I've been wanting to beat myself up for a long time. I have no scruples except when it comes to my clients' best interests. Would you like me to sleep with you?

ASHRAF. Barry.

BARRY. I don't even know your sexual preference. I know I'm not much to look at, but I'm willing. Even Cantwell would get on his knees and blow you. That's how much we care for your career.

ASHRAF. Let go.

BARRY. Or Peggy, if you're straight. She'd do it as one last favor if I threw in a good severance package. There are so many people out there who are looking out for you.

ASHRAF. Please let go.

BARRY. No.

ASHRAF. Let go.

BARRY. No. (*Barry drops to Ashraf's foot and clings onto it.*)

ASHRAF. Get off me.

BARRY. No no no. No. Not without a yes. I'm groveling. Isn't that what you want? I'm doing it. I'm kissing your foot. (*He kisses his foot.*)

ASHRAF. Stop it.

BARRY. Say it.

ASHRAF. Barry.

BARRY. Say "yes." (*Continues to kiss his foot.*)

ASHRAF. (*He moves towards his bag, dragging Barry along the way.*) Barry, for chrissakes. Get a hold of yourself. Where's your dignity?

BARRY. I don't have any. I'll never let go. I'll never stop fighting for you.

ASHRAF. Would you just — (*Barry bites into Ashraf's ankle. Ashraf cries out in pain.*) Aaggh. Ow. Ow. Barry: (*Ashraf tries to disengage but Barry continues biting.*) You're hurting me! (*Ashraf falls to the floor. Peggy enters. She stops for a second to take in the scene. Ashraf and Barry freeze. She walks to a chair and retrieves an item left behind by Cassandra. She stops again to look at Barry still clinging to Ashraf's foot. Slight beat.)*

BARRY. Can't you see I'm in the middle of something.

PEGGY. I'm handing in my notice.

BARRY. Great.

PEGGY. This agency has never really appreciated my qualifications.

BARRY. I doubt it. Goodbye. *(Peggy turns and heads for the door.)* Wait. Could you put in a good word with your new employer.

PEGGY. *(As she exits.)* Fuck off.

BARRY. Fair enough. *(Peggy has closed the door behind her. Barry and Ashraf remain on the floor. Barry sidles up next to Ashraf.)* So. What's it going to be? The future? Bright, resplendent, which waits for no one. Not even the talented among us. Or the slag heap of has-beens, that's ever-ravenous and would love to have you. *(Slight beat.)*

ASHRAF. I'm going to hate myself in the morning. — Either way.

BARRY. Yes, but hatred with a good goal that benefits others is emotion well-spent. And is love by any other name.

ASHRAF. Barry.

BARRY. Anything.

ASHRAF. Shut up.

BARRY. Consider it done. *(Blackout.)*

End of Play

PROPERTY LIST

Screenplay
Door key
Cigar box
Briefcase
Calculator
Wrist watch
Intercom
Magazines
Playboy Magazine
Packet of powder
Set of keys (2)
Cell phones (2)
Gadgets
Box of tissues
Paperweight
Tripod
Video camera
Bag
Handgun
Keffiyeh
Bottled waters
Cigarette
Lighter
Hand mirror
Purse

NEW PLAYS

★ **CLYBOURNE PARK by Bruce Norris.** WINNER OF THE 2011 PULITZER PRIZE AND 2012 TONY AWARD. Act One takes place in 1959 as community leaders try to stop the sale of a home to a black family. Act Two is set in the same house in the present day as the now predominantly African-American neighborhood battles to hold its ground. "Vital, sharp-witted and ferociously smart." –*NY Times.* "A theatrical treasure…Indisputably, uproariously funny." –*Entertainment Weekly.* [4M, 3W] ISBN: 978-0-8222-2697-0

★ **WATER BY THE SPOONFUL by Quiara Alegría Hudes.** WINNER OF THE 2012 PULITZER PRIZE. A Puerto Rican veteran is surrounded by the North Philadelphia demons he tried to escape in the service. "This is a very funny, warm, and yes uplifting play." –*Hartford Courant.* "The play is a combination poem, prayer and app on how to cope in an age of uncertainty, speed and chaos." –*Variety.* [4M, 3W] ISBN: 978-0-8222-2716-8

★ **RED by John Logan.** WINNER OF THE 2010 TONY AWARD. Mark Rothko has just landed the biggest commission in the history of modern art. But when his young assistant, Ken, gains the confidence to challenge him, Rothko faces the agonizing possibility that his crowning achievement could also become his undoing. "Intense and exciting." –*NY Times.* "Smart, eloquent entertainment." –*New Yorker.* [2M] ISBN: 978-0-8222-2483-9

★ **VENUS IN FUR by David Ives.** Thomas, a beleaguered playwright/director, is desperate to find an actress to play Vanda, the female lead in his adaptation of the classic sadomasochistic tale *Venus in Fur.* "Ninety minutes of good, kinky fun." –*NY Times.* "A fast-paced journey into one man's entrapment by a clever, vengeful female." –*Associated Press.* [1M, 1W] ISBN: 978-0-8222-2603-1

★ **OTHER DESERT CITIES by Jon Robin Baitz.** Brooke returns home to Palm Springs after a six-year absence and announces that she is about to publish a memoir dredging up a pivotal and tragic event in the family's history—a wound they don't want reopened. "Leaves you feeling both moved and gratifyingly sated." –*NY Times.* "A genuine pleasure." –*NY Post.* [2M, 3W] ISBN: 978-0-8222-2605-5

★ **TRIBES by Nina Raine.** Billy was born deaf into a hearing family and adapts brilliantly to his family's unconventional ways, but it's not until he meets Sylvia, a young woman on the brink of deafness, that he finally understands what it means to be understood. "A smart, lively play." –*NY Times.* "[A] bright and boldly provocative drama." –*Associated Press.* [3M, 2W] ISBN: 978-0-8222-2751-9

DRAMATISTS PLAY SERVICE, INC.
440 Park Avenue South, New York, NY 10016 212-683-8960 Fax 212-213-1539
postmaster@dramatists.com   www.dramatists.com